I Can See

by Cameron Grieft
illustrated by Eva Vagreti

Core Decodable 5

Mc Graw Hill Education

Bothell, WA • Chicago, IL • Columbus, OH • New York, NY

MHEonline.com

Copyright © 2015 McGraw-Hill Education

All rights reserved. No part of this publication may be reproduced or distributed in any form or by any means, or stored in a database or retrieval system, without the prior written consent of McGraw-Hill Education, including, but not limited to, network storage or transmission, or broadcast for distance learning.

Send all inquiries to:
McGraw-Hill Education
8787 Orion Place
Columbus, OH 43240

ISBN: 978-0-02-135444-3
MHID: 0-02-135444-8

Printed in the United States of America.

2 3 4 5 6 7 8 9 DOC 20 19 18 17 16 15

I can see the [bus].

I can see the ▢ on the ▢.

4   bus driver   bus

I can see a boy on the bus.

I can see [boys] on the [bus].

I can see girls on the bus.

I can see the ▢.

school